Nobody Calls It SIN Anymore

Fr. Kenneth J. Roberts

Our Sunday Visitor Publishing Division
Our Sunday Visitor, Inc.
Huntington, Indiana 46750

This book is dedicated to Our Blessed
Mother and to the many people who have
encouraged me with their prayerful support.

Acknowledgments

To my editor, Anna Marie Waters, and to my proofreader, Judith Horvath, thank you.

Table of Contents

Preface 9

Chapter One:
    Spiritual Warfare 12

Chapter Two:
    The Ten Commandments 31

Chapter Three:
    The Greatest Commandment 86

Chapter Four:
    "Whose Sins You Shall Forgive" 93

Chapter Five:
    "My Peace I Leave You" 105

Preface

Lamb of God, You take away the sins of the world, have mercy on us. Next to the words at the Consecration, *"This is My Body. . . . This is My Blood,"* I believe the *Agnus Dei* (Lamb of God) that we say at every Mass is the most powerful. Think about it. Jesus took away *our* sins! But Jesus, the Man, didn't do it with a wave of His hand, or a nod of His head. Not hardly. Jesus gave His life in a bloody sacrifice.

I believe that if all of us sat before a crucifix and meditated on this ultimate act of love, there would be no need to write, or preach, about sin. If we have any heart at all, we would be compelled to live according to the Ten Commandments, not out of fear of hell, but out of love for the Lord Who gave His Life to wash away our sins in His Blood. Through His sacrifice and death, eternal life is ours to share with our heavenly Father.

But the world pulls us away from the cross, and the image of the crucified Christ is obscured by the modern day "fruit of the tree": power, wealth, comfort, and pleasure. And just as the world tempts us, the world is equally eager to absolve us, because "nobody calls it *sin* anymore."

Ruthless behavior is no more than a character flaw. Fornication is a mutual act of consent that doesn't hurt anybody. Adultery is a meaningful expression of love. Violence is a result of bad upbringing. Cheating an employer is winning against the establishment. Gossip is innocent conversation. Stealing is no more than satisfying a need. Murder of the unborn is freedom of choice. And somewhere amid all these things, that inner voice known as conscience is losing its volume and becoming more difficult to be heard. The question is: Do any of the above bring peace?

Never.

We know that doing the will of the Father brings peace, so while the modern world searches for this peace in material things, it overlooks the formula that was given to Moses and written in stone — the Ten Commandments. The truth is, we don't want to be told "Thou shall not" because it means being told "No" to the things we foolishly pursue under the misguided notion that we will be happy if we *do* this, or *have* that.

Meanwhile, Holy Mother Church, like a voice in the wilderness competing with the din of materialism, screams out for our attention, reminding us that sin does exist. She dusts off the tablets and holds them before us crying out, "Here's the formula for a good life, not only in this world but for all eternity!" Reminding us all about the "*Thou shall nots*" makes her unpopular, and indeed, that holds true for anyone who tries to take up her cause. It is for that precise reason that the need to preach and teach the Ten Commandments is so demanding today. I pray that the following pages will enlighten the confused, inform the un-churched, and reinforce the commitment of the faithful.

It's not enough to learn and discern the Ten Commandments, but rather, by focusing on our crucified Christ, following God's laws is no more than a response to His love. Through meditating on Jesus' redemptive act, we will not be moti-vated by reward or punishment, but by love. Like St. Paul's, our motto will be, "the love of God im-pels us . . ."(2 Cor 5:14).

Chapter One:
Spiritual Warfare

The Disguises of Sin

Sin comes in many shapes and sizes, and often it is hard to recognize because we can't get beyond the disguise. For some, the disguise is power and affluence that promise happiness. For others, it's sexual pleasure without respect for ourselves or others. And too often, sin is disguised as something good. Who would argue with a man who wants to support his family and offer his children the advantages of living in a nice neighborhood and going to good schools? That's a *good* thing, but suppose he has to rob a bank to do it. Or what about the young unmarried couple who has fallen in love and wants to share everything with each other, even their bodies? Seems like a good thing, but remember, the sixth commandment forbids fornication.

Sin is also disguised by language. Who would deny a woman the right to choose what happens to her body? But when her decision results in the murder of her unborn child, that's a direct violation of the fifth commandment, "You shall not kill."

And who would not want to ease the suffering of a terminally ill person who is wracked with pain? We even attach a good name to the act of euthanasia: *mercy* killing. Are we not directed to have *mercy*? Also, the word "virgin" when not applied to olive oil or wool, is generally used to depict something unnatural, or it's used to get a few laughs. I remember when it was a virtue appropriate to all unmarried persons. Today, the loss of virginity, especially before marriage, is the plot for many dramas and the subject for much distorted humor.

There seems to be a trend that if it's a popular thing, if "everybody's doing it," it must be OK. I challenge anyone to sit down to an evening of television watching, whether it's sitcoms or dramas, and not see at least one instance of adultery or fornication. In the meantime, we are becoming desensitized to sin because "nobody calls it *sin* anymore."

The marketing of sin makes victims of our children. How can they make the right choices without the proper instruction and role models? If a young boy's role model is some so-called hero who employs the martial arts to cripple or kill an aggressor, is that a good thing? What about the little girl who wants to be just like the main character on one of the popular sitcoms? How many chaste single women do you recall watching on prime-time television? Just recently, a sitcom with already high ratings took on a new twist by allowing the main character to reveal she's a lesbian. She's witty, honest, and a good friend, so what's wrong with little girls wanting to be just like her? Before I am accused of gay-bashing, let me hasten to add that chastity must be employed regardless of sexual preference. But offering the prospect of alternative lifestyles to young people carries a grave responsibility, because regardless of how social justice falsely clamors, homosexual unions are not in God's plan.

We are living in a world that claims to want to preserve our environment for future generations, and certainly that is a worthwhile cause. It's good to worry about the air we breathe, the preservation of the rain forests, the elimination of toxic waste, and the damage to the ozone. Ecology is an important issue among social activists and politicians, but what about the inner ecology? We are polluting our young people's minds by glorifying sin. Children need clean entertainment as much as clean air to grow spiritually. I'm amused by the signs that say "Clean up America" while young people trudge through the piles of psychological litter that clutter our country in the entertainment media.

There is such incongruity today. We see many celebrities taking up the cause for children's rights, while the same people insist on legalized abortion. But abortion is the ultimate child abuse! It's also quite interesting that many of the same people who demonstrate *against* abortion support capital punishment, and vice versa. Then we have Mr. or Mrs. Corporate America, who claim to be God-fearing Christians but whose job it is to eliminate blue collar workers while enhancing his or her own salary to astronomical proportions. I also found it quite amusing that Congress bickered over the minimum wage law but never batted an eye when raising their own salaries. Furthermore, there are many who claim to live by the creed "Honesty is the best policy" but then cheat on their income taxes.

Since we're talking about sin wearing so many disguises, let's focus on the costume designer, the devil himself. This book cannot discuss the subject of sin without enlightening the reader about Satan, the author of sin. I must preface this by sharing something with you. I have a friend who always sprinkles holy water on her computer whenever she is writing or editing anything that refers to the devil. She began this practice after she experienced mysterious complications and obstacles while dealing with the subject of diabolical intervention. There is nothing superstitious about guarding oneself against the devil. He never wants to be exposed or recognized. He loves camouflage and denial of his existence because it gives him a distinct advantage. Denial of the devil is his greatest weapon, and whenever we seek to expose his battle plan, we must be prepared.

The devil said "No" to God, and he urges us to do the same. He makes us vulnerable to his advances by spreading confusion, not peace. He makes an evil appear to be something good. And he always has his army of greed and power to flank his attack. But not to worry, we have our own strategy and a Leader who will always render the devil's invasion ineffective. Our Leader is more powerful, and His promise is life, not death. He gives peace, not confusion. He pours out love, not hate. He offers comfort, not despair. He has given us the weapons to fight off the attack of the devil — prayer and the sacraments, as well as His Ten Commandments.

I find it troubling that more and more Satanic cults are springing up around this country and throughout the world, yet we hear less and less about the devil from our pulpits. Perhaps that's because the devil is an unpopular subject, and perhaps because many deny his existence. But

Scripture affirms the existence of the devil over and over. This is brought forth in definite terms, and the editor of *Our Sunday Visitor's Catholic Encyclopedia* has made it very simple for us to research. The following is taken directly from the encyclopedia, pages 304-305:

Devil

In the Old Testament, the term is always used with an article "*the* satan." The LXX (Septuagint, [the Greek translation of the Hebrew Old Testament]) renders the word "diabolos," which means accurser or a military adversary.

. . . . In the New Testament, there is no distinction drawn between "diabolos" and "satanas." Satan is the strong one (Mt 12:29), the evil one (Mt 13:19) and the prince of the world (Jn 12:31). . . . He tempts with designs (1 Cor 7:5) and deceit (Eph 6:11). He disguises himself as an angel of light (2 Cor 11:14) and seduces some of the faithful (1 Tm 5:15). All the kingdoms of the world are under his power (Lk 4:6), and his power is frustrated until his time (Lk 4:13). The Antichrist comes with the active power of Satan (2 Thes 2:9), is bound at the millennium in the pit (Rv 20:2), and is released to work for destruction until the end of the world (Rv 20:7). He is identified with the serpent of the creation story and is associated with the great dragon of ancient mythology. Satan remains subject to the power of God and is ultimately overcome by Jesus. The sons of the devil are those who do not love the brothers and do not act in righteousness. Heresy refers to "the deep things of Satan" (Rv 2:24).

The devil is not just a personification of evil, and the existence of the devil must not be denied. The doctrine of the devil points to the calamitous situation faced by humanity, which is not entirely our doing and can only be remedied by God. The doctrine of the devil affirms that there is an evil domain into which humanity has been plunged and is redeemed from that only by God and human freedom contributes to this situation.

Dogmatic theology and the Second Vatican Council are reserved about the power of the devil over human actions. Despite his power, he is a finite creature, and his power is circumscribed by the power of God.

The devil does not work alone, and this also is made very clear and easy to research when we refer to *Our Sunday Visitor's Catholic Encyclopedia:*

Devil and Evil Spirits

Evil spirits are fallen angels, among whom one — called the Devil or Satan — is traditionally held to exercise leadership. The fallen angels are those purely spiritual beings who, after being created by God and endowed with grace, failed to respond to God's love and turned away from Him (2 Pt 2:4; cf Mt 25:41; Jude 6). According to Christian Tradition, their sin was one of pride: They preferred to usurp or claim as their own a likeness to God that could only be received as a gift. As purely spiritual beings who do not require time and reflection to come to knowledge and decision, their refusal of God's love was irrevocable. Their situation is thus comparable to the post-mortem state of unrepentant human sinners.

Although they have lost supernatural grace, the fallen angels retain the powers of purely spiritual beings. They deploy these powers in a variety of ways to obstruct the fulfillment of God's plan and to block the progress of human beings toward bliss. They do this not simply by tempting people to sin, but chiefly by fostering despair and unrepentance in sinners who otherwise might turn with confidence to the sure mercy of God.

According to the Scriptures, the Devil and the fallen angels were active in bringing about the passion and death of Christ, and in general in striving to thwart His saving mission in the world. As great as their powers are, they are now under the dominion of Christ, who has imparted to His Church the power to forgive sins and to drive out demons. While Divine Providence permits them a limited scope of activity, they are powerless to block in any decisive way the consummation of the economy of salvation, the movement of all things toward God (p. 305).

Just in case there are those of you who have been misinformed that the teachings of the Church about the devil have been diluted since Vatican II, refer to The new *Catechism of the Catholic Church*: "Satan or the devil and the other demons are fallen angels who have freely refused to serve God and His plan. Their choice against

God is definitive. They try to associate man in their revolt against God" (414).

We poor creatures are the target of the devil in his revolt against God so it's no wonder that we are surrounded by temptations. But don't be dismayed, God is more powerful, and He loves us. Armed with the knowledge that through Baptism we became children of God, we can rest assured that like any good father, God will be there to protect us.

"For you, O Lord, are good and forgiving, abounding in kindness to all who call upon you. Hearken, O LORD, to my prayer and attend to the sound of my pleading. In the day of my distress I call upon you, for you will answer me" (Ps 86:5-7).

In All Good Conscience

"Let your conscience be your guide," can give you a lot of latitude and get you in a whole lot of trouble if you haven't sought to form a good conscience. All of us, if we are psychologically sound, have an inner gauge that allows us to judge right from wrong. But unfortunately, conscience sometimes falls prey to rationalization, that process whereby we justify our actions when we act contrary to what our better judgment tells us.

Nobody wants to admit that he or she is

choosing an evil over good, and it's hard to imagine that anyone could have the courage, or contempt, to say "No" to God, yet "who among us is without sin?" It's that rationalization process that takes over and causes us to give in to temptation. Rationalization is certain to lead to sin if we have not formed a strong conscience.

Our conscience can be compared to a muscle which will certainly atrophy and grow weak if it is not exercised. Focusing on God, prayer, the sacraments, the study of God's commandments, and living by the teachings of the Church are the spiritual exercises that are essential to form a good, strong conscience. It's how we respond to God's call to holiness.

In today's world, the voice of our conscience must compete with the roar of the media that glorifies materialism and pleasure. We're so saturated with it that we become desensitized to it. When instructing young people about purity, invariably when the subject of premarital sex is addressed, I can count on hearing, "I don't see how *that* can be a sin, after all, we aren't hurting anybody." But the kids aren't totally to blame for that kind of attitude when you consider that so much of their entertainment focuses on sexual subjects. It is for that reason that parents and religious educators have a rough time today teaching what is and is not acceptable behavior. We look into the eyes of these young people who seem to be sarcastically saying, "Yeah, right!" They are certain that we are just plain old-fashioned and don't understand. But what they don't understand is that theirs is not the first generation that has had to deal with hormones; we all went through the questioning and learning process, and with the proper guidance and prayer, we got our priorities together and we trusted God to be there to get us through temptation. The biggest difference is that contemporary society has become so permissive. It's the *me, my, I* philosophy that demands no boundaries in the pursuit of gratification, whether it concerns wealth, fame, popularity, sex, drugs, alcohol, or power.

Another line we hear from the young people when they are reminded that certain behavior is sinful is, "That's no big deal." But every time we excuse ourselves from any sin, mortal or venial, it *is* a "big deal." True, venial sin doesn't represent eternal death, but it predisposes us to greater sin. It can cause our muscle of conscience to grow weaker and lose resistance.

It's not difficult to understand why there's so much confusion about sin, when first of all we deny it, then if we do acknowledge it, we are told to absolve ourselves. I remember a conversation with a psychiatrist friend of mine who said that one of the lines he heard over and over in his classes was, "Guilt is a useless emotion." Certainly it is useless, if we refuse to accept God's forgiveness and become obsessive about our transgressions, but I hasten to say a little "healthy" guilt is a good thing when it encompasses remorse — true sorrow for our sins. That's where we Catholics have an edge. We can receive in the Sacrament of Penance what many individuals receive after hours and hours in therapy.

When our conscience is good and firm, we will be wise enough to avoid the occasions of sin — those persons, places, or things that tempt us. We should be careful to choose wholesome entertainment, and be selective about how we spend our time. "An idle mind is the devil's workshop," is an old saying that is really quite profound. And just as fertile a field for the devil to wage his battle is a lax conscience, for "If we say, 'We are without sin,' we deceive ourselves, and the truth is not in us. If we acknowledge our sins, he is faithful and just and will forgive our sins and cleanse us from every wrongdoing" (1 Jn 1:8-9).

Temptation and Sin

It's interesting to note that the *American Heritage Dictionary* defines sin as, "a deliberate disobedience to the known will of God," and "a condition of estrangement from God resulting from such a disobedience." Although this is a secular publication, it doesn't differ much from what we learned as children, that sin is deliberately breaking God's law.

In simple language, sin is saying "No" to God. When you really think about it, that takes a lot of guts. Who is bold enough to say "No" to God? We all are, if we knowingly choose what is contrary to His commandments. But we have a way of rationalizing our actions. Never would we admit to choosing evil because quite often evil is disguised as good. That's where the devil comes in and nudges us with temptation. Even Jesus was tempted in the desert (Mt 4:1-11), but He didn't give in. It's important to keep in mind that temptation is *not* a sin, only a prelude to one, if we give in to it.

There's real warfare going on: good versus evil. The temptations are great because sin is camouflaged in so many ways. If you have any doubts, check out some of the number-one shows on network television that are extremely popular with young people. One such show built a whole season's subplots around two of the main characters going to bed with each other. There was never the slightest indication that anything but good was about to happen when these two finally fornicated. This show is aired in prime time when so many children are watching. How can they help but be influenced by this total disregard of one of God's commandments?

Also, violence is a form of entertainment with box-office appeal. It's difficult to distinguish the "good guys" from the "bad guys" when both sides inflict pain and death. In the meantime, we and especially our children are becoming desensitized to the horrors of violent behavior without realizing it. The media are certainly making the devil's job easier! So, we poor mortals are struggling along trying to discern what is of God, and what is evil. And that, dear friends, is where our conscience comes in.

Again, let's call upon a secular definition of conscience: "The awareness of a moral or ethical aspect to one's conduct together with the urge to prefer right over wrong." So, we have a definite goal. It's absolutely essential that we form a *good conscience* when we make our choices. But the stakes are higher than just right or wrong — we're talking about good or evil; peace or torment; hope or despair; harmony or chaos, and yes, even heaven or hell.

As children of our loving God the Father, we have all that we need to persevere and be victorious over evil. We need only to use the guidelines God has given to us and follow His commandments. As Catholics, we have additional fortification over evil in the power of the sacraments. Prayer, Mass, and Confession are the tools that build a good and strong conscience. Love of God is what compels us to take advantage of them.

Two Kinds of Sin

Original sin was handed down to us from the first human beings, who rejected God's creation of a world of perfect love and harmony. As children, we learned from the figurative account in Genesis that it was the woman who was tempted by the serpent (the devil) and ate of the forbidden fruit. Adam also fell through the temptation. That act of turning away from God brought with it disharmony and a disposition to sin. That was our legacy from the sin of the first human beings. It is believed that all of mankind has the mark of original sin with the exception of Mary, the Mother of God.

The doctrine of the Immaculate Conception states that: "The Blessed Virgin Mary was preserved, in the first instant of her conception, by a singular grace and privilege of God omnipotent and because of the merits of Jesus Christ, the Savior of the human race, was free from all stain of original sin" (from the declaration of the dogma by Pope Pius IX, December 8, 1854).

Original sin is washed away by the Sacrament of Baptism.

Actual sin is a deliberate turning away from God. Unlike original sin which we can't do anything about, actual sin is our personal choice to disobey God's law. We must want to do it, know how serious it is, and then, with full knowledge, commit the sin.

Sin predisposes us to more sin. In other words, the more we do it, the easier it becomes, and before long we *choose* not to even think of it as a sin any longer.

Two Types of Actual Sin

Mortal Sin is a grievous offense against the laws of God. It is called "mortal" because it is deadly to our souls. If we are in mortal sin, we need the Sacrament of Reconciliation to be absolved.

Venial Sin is a less serious offense against the laws of God. It called "venial" because it is more easily forgiven and pardoned. Venial sins can be forgiven through an act of sincere contrition.

St. John says, "True, all wrongdoing is sin but, there is sin that is not deadly [mortal]" (1 Jn 5:17). This is one passage from Scripture to support the Church's teaching regarding mortal and venial sin.

The teachings of Vatican II have not changed in regard to the degrees of sin. In the following three paragraphs, the new *Catechism* describes the Church's teaching:

"To choose deliberately — that is, both knowing it and willing it — something gravely contrary to the divine law and to the ultimate end of man is to commit a mortal sin. This destroys in us the charity without which eternal beatitude is impossible. Unrepented, it brings eternal death"(1874).

"Venial sin constitutes a moral disorder that is reparable by charity, which it allows to subsist in us" (1875).

"The repetition of sins — even venial ones — engenders vices, among which are the capital sins" (1876).

The Seven Deadly Sins

The seven deadly sins are also referred to as *capital* sins because they're the vices that lead to other sins. They are: pride, avarice, envy, anger, lust, intemperance, and sloth.

Pride is excessive esteem for oneself over esteem for God.

Avarice is an inordinate desire for material things or personal worldly honor.

Envy or jealousy is begrudging others' accomplishments or possessions.

Anger arouses hostile feelings toward others, destroying peace and harmony.

Lust is the desire of pleasures of the flesh.

Intemperance is a lack of restraint in our desire for food, drink, alcohol, or any activity we engage in without moderation.

Sloth is not striving for spiritual growth, resulting in a diminished love for God and an increase of love for pleasure. Very often, this vice often leads to despair.

Summary

Sin is saying "No" to God.

Temptation is not a sin, only a prelude to one.

We can acquire a good conscience through prayer and the sacraments.

There are two kinds of sin, original and actual.

The two types of actual sin are mortal (deadly) and venial (more easily pardoned).

The seven deadly sins are vices that are the root of all sins against God's laws.

Chapter Two:

The Ten Commandments

Perhaps it would be appropriate at this point to make a simple observation about why God gave us His Ten Commandments. Remember, He is our Father, and like any father, He wants what is best for us. The head of every family sets down rules that will serve the best interest of all family members. If each member only lives according to his or her personal rule, then there's chaos.

Most people look upon rules or laws as merely restrictions, and so we have a tendency to rebel. God didn't give us His rules to enslave us, but rather to set us free to be all that we can be in His image. Patterning our lives according to His rules will bring us the greatest reward of all, eternal life. It's what our Father wants for us. Keeping the Ten Commandments is simply responding to His love.

The Ten Commandments of God are also referred to as "the Decalogue," meaning the ten words of God given to Moses on Mount Sinai. It's God's guidelines for us to live according to

His plan and a formula for all of us to live together in peace and harmony.

Since sin is saying "no" to God's commandments, it's essential that we understand just what the commandments mean. It may have been a while since many of you studied the Ten Commandments, so consider this a mini refresher course. For those of you who are taking a closer look at the commandments for the first time, remember that it is absolutely essential that we know God's rules to form a good conscience.

The following Ten Commandments are in accordance with the Roman Catholic listing. Protestant and Eastern Orthodox religions number them differently. I, along with other traditional religious educators, consider it a true blessing that the new *Catechism* leaves no room for conjecture about how the commandments should be instructed. It is very precise on the teachings that pertain to each of the Ten Commandments, as is Our Lord: "Teacher, what good must I do to gain eternal life?" Jesus answered the young man by saying, ". . . If you wish to enter into life, keep the commandments" (Mt 19:16-17).

The Ten Commandments

I. I am the LORD, your God; you shall not have strange gods before Me.

II. You shall not take the name of the LORD, your God, in vain.

III. Remember to keep holy the LORD's day.

IV. Honor your father and your mother.

V. You shall not kill.

VI. You shall not commit adultery.

VII. You shall not steal.

VIII. You shall not bear false witness against your neighbor.

IX. You shall not covet your neighbor's spouse.

X. You shall not covet your neighbor's goods.

The first three commandments are directed toward God, and the other seven are directed toward our relationships with others. Many preachers remind us that God gave us His commandments, not His *suggestions*. To live our lives to the fullest, we are called to obedience, not speculation. Our Lord made Himself very clear about His rules. We're the ones who dilute them with rationalization in order to bend those rules to suit our own needs.

1. I am the LORD, your God, You shall have no strange gods before me

The first commandment calls us to worship and serve God. "'The Lord, your God, shall you worship and him alone shall you serve'" (Mt 4:10). We worship God through prayer and virtuous acts. We Catholics have the perfect prayer in the Liturgy of the Mass. Another wonderful advantage we have is the privilege of spending time before the Blessed Sacrament. I wonder if the majority of Catholics really understand how generous Holy Mother Church has been to its members. Can you think of any other denominations that have a prayer service every day and keep the doors open for private prayer? Perhaps, in rural areas, Catholics are not as blessed as in larger cities, but for the most part, a Catholic can attend Mass everyday without traveling great distances.

The first commandment also embraces the virtues of faith, hope, and charity. **Faith** calls us to be vigilant and prudent and to learn our faith so that we may defend it. **Hope** urges us to trust in God alone as our salvation. **Charity** obliges us to love God first, and to love others for the love of God.

Sins against the First Commandment

Sins against faith are apostasy, heresy, and indifference. **Apostasy** is the rejection of the Faith by a baptized Catholic. **Heresy** is a willful denial of the official teachings of the Church. **Indifference** is the refusal to give worship to God, or the refusal to accept one's obligation to worship God.

Sins against charity are hatred of God and hatred of others.

Sins against hope are presumption and despair.

The sins against faith and charity pretty much speak for themselves. But the sins against hope, **presumption and despair,** are a bit more complicated. By presumption, a person trusts that he can be saved merely by his own efforts and without God's help, or that God will save him no matter what he does. In contrast, when a person sins through despair, he refuses to trust in a loving God who has pledged to save him. So, what we have here is this distinction: Presumption is overestimating our own power and despair is underestimating God's power and mercy.

The sins against the first commandment often result in **agnosticism** and even **atheism.** An agnostic doesn't deny that God exists, but hasn't been satisfied with the proof that He does. An atheist denies the very existence of God. Can you imagine such a lonely state? Where do we go when life seems intolerable? What do we do when we feel so helpless? And where is hope? If all we can count on is what we see with our eyes, hear with our ears, and feel with our hearts, then what lies beyond this life? Death becomes an abrupt, foreboding end. Love is merely a feeling for someone, or something, and we all know how fickle feelings are. Life is a series of happy times and sad times, nothing more.

But God-believers have everything to look forward to — eternal life. Death is merely a passage to a greater life. Love is more than a feeling, it is a virtue. And life is God's gift to us, and how we use our time here on earth is our gift to Him.

Idolatry

Idolatry is another sin against the first commandment and it sometimes conjures up an image of a pagan culture worshiping an image of a calf, or a mountain, or as Scripture says, "a graven image." But we have made gods for ourselves in modern times — we have the god of wealth, the god of power, the god of pleasure, and the god of vanity. Anything that takes priority over God in our lives is a "strange god" we put before Him.

One can't help but wonder if God doesn't sit

back and say, "Here they go again — how many times do I have to show them?" Even within our own faith, we see "strange gods" arising. In the extreme feminist movement within the Church, there is a ritual that calls upon the "goddess of the cosmos." And our God, the Father, is also referred to as Mother God. Talk about confusion! Those who follow this extreme movement have made a "strange god" of equal rights and they have forgotten that we are all equal in the eyes of God. Are they seeking equality or is their "strange god" the god of power?

God knows His children, and His commandments are as contemporary today as they were during the time of Moses. The people are different, but the transgressions are the same.

Fundamentalists have accused Catholics of having idols because of our use of statues and images. Some actually believe that we worship the statues. How absurd! Statues, religious art, and symbols are merely devotional tools. I can't imagine anything more futile than worshiping a statue. Some fundamentalists object to the very casting of statues as producing graven images, but many of these same people will visit the Statue of Liberty. Why? Because that statue represents something about the United States. God knows how many immigrants who, after suffering the ordeals of long voyages to live in a land of freedom, sang out in joy at the sight of that statue in New York Harbor. Did they worship the statue? No, but they revered what it represented, freedom to live without tyranny and also freedom to worship.

Also, Catholics are often accused of making an idol of Mary, the Mother of Jesus. We are criticized for referring to her as Our Blessed Mother, but that's what she is to us. We believe that Jesus gave us His mother as He hung on the cross when He said to John, ". . . Behold, your mother" (Jn 19:27). Mary, as Mother of the Church and model of all Christians, certainly deserves our respect. Her role as intercessor and prayer partner has long been recognized by the Church.

Many who object to our use of statues of Our Blessed Mother and the saints will have the same images in a Christmas creche scene in December, but they will call it idolatry if they see them displayed the other eleven months of the year. In neither case is it against the first commandment unless the statues are adored and worshiped.

Superstition

Superstition is giving honor or power that belongs to God to any creature or thing. Even some prayer practices, though good in themselves, become superstitious when we attach some supernatural phenomenum to them. Chain letters are a good example of that. Have you ever received a chain letter requesting that you say some designated prayers and then contact ten more people instructing them to do the same? In return for this effort, you are granted some special favor. Often a few lines are included about how someone who did not continue the chain fell into bad times. This is not a legitimate way to spread a prayer practice or devotion.

We must never ascribe supernatural power to things such as lucky charms or crystals, and we are forbidden to believe in fortune tellers, seances, psychics, Tarot cards, Ouija boards, horoscopes, or to dabble in anything of the occult. Also, we must be on guard against an avalanche of New Age theology which has even invaded our Church.

Satanism

Satanism is the worship of the devil. Perhaps many Catholics feel that this abhorrent practice is so remote from our everyday world that it hardly warrants mentioning. If only that were true: Contrary to what most average people believe, Satanism is on the rise in this country and it has touched our rural areas as much as our big cities. It's been discovered on our college campuses, in our military, and right in the middle of our cozy suburbs. Devil worship is more than a subject for thriller movies — it's a practice that is gaining momentum throughout our nation. To deny the existence of the devil and satanism is to allow the evil one more power on the spiritual battlefield.

In spiritual warfare, as in any warfare, the enemy is often camouflaged so he won't be recognized. Unawareness and denial create a fertile field for the devil to flourish. Indifference to the first commandment, which calls us to put God first in our lives, allows the devil to move in closer and hit his target.

I don't want to give the devil and evil any more space in this book, but it's difficult to avoid the topic when "sin" is the subject. So, in as simple language as possible, keep this in mind. The devil does exist. He is out there and gaining more followers. He often is disguised as good. He's a strategist — don't underestimate him. But don't overestimate him either. God is more powerful, and unlike the devil, God loves us!

Prayer

The first commandment calls for an obligation to prayer and worship of the one true God. It isn't enough that we believe God exists; we must come to know Him. The best way to be better acquainted with someone is to spend time with them. So it is with God. Through Scripture reading and prayer, we provide the essential nourishment for the growth of our spiritual lives.

To maintain a healthy body, we eat food regularly because without the proper nourishment, our physical well-being would surely fail. If we spent as much time feeding our souls as we spend feeding our bodies, what powerful Christians we'd become!

Most of us consume three meals a day and perhaps a snack in between if we're hungry. If we only consume junk food, it may temporarily satisfy our hunger, but not only are we not receiving the proper nourishment to have a healthy body, we could be absorbing foods that are dangerous to our health. Today, when there's so much emphasis on watching our cholesterol intake to keep our arteries from becoming blocked, many of us have begun reading the labels for information about fat and cholesterol. If we're seriously trying to maintain and improve our health, we will consume only those foods that are not dangerous to our health.

Our spiritual health is no different. Beware of junk-food spirituality. Read the label. Look for an endorsement, usually found at the front of the book, that alerts the reader that nothing in the material is in conflict with matters of faith and morals. Today, when the religious market is saturated with New Age spirituality, be picky about what you consume intellectually and spiritually.

In pursuit of physical fitness, we put our bodies through all kinds of strenuous exercises, and this requires a good deal of our time if we do it regularly. For spiritual fitness, take time to work out before the Blessed Sacrament by bending your knees, then be still and feel His Divine Presence.

Summary

The first commandment calls us to trust in God and offer worship to Him alone.

Idolatry is not only the adoration of graven images, it's putting other people, things, or causes before God.

Superstition is giving supernatural power and honor to any creature or thing.

Satanism, worship of the devil, does exist and is growing throughout the world.

Prayer and worship are vital for our spiritual well-being.

2. You shall not take the name of the LORD, your God, in vain

God is all-holy and His name is holy; we must never use it in an unholy way. The name of God must never be used except to praise, honor, bless, and glorify Him or to call upon Him in prayer.

Blasphemy

Blasphemy, in secular terms, means abusive language. In Scripture, blasphemy is any abusive and irreverent language toward God or anything holy. Too often, many people use the name of God as an expletive, such as, "God! Did you see that?" Now, they are not talking to God in prayer, so they are using His name in vain.

Many of our slang expressions have evolved from what was once blasphemous expressions. In my own country, England, the word "bloody" is used quite frequently in conversation, but most modern Brits don't realize that it was originally a blasphemy. It is a corruption of the expression "By Our Lady," just as the Irish expression "Be Jeebers" is a corruption of the expression "By Jesus." Here in the States, the popular slang, "Gosh" and "Golly" are used do denote surprise or awe, but they evolved as an alternative to the word "God." "Darn" is an alternative to "damn," and "Gee" and "Gee Whiz" are alternatives to "Jesus."

People using these slang expressions are not guilty of blasphemy because the slang is not used with the intention of abusing the name of God. Unfortunately, there are many who use the name of God so indiscriminately that it becomes a very undesirable habit.

The best put-down of blasphemy I ever witnessed was at a rather large social gathering where an obnoxious drunk continued to intersperse his very loud conversation with the name of Jesus Christ. The hostess, a very refined and proper lady, glared at him and said, "Name dropper!" This broke the embarrassed silence of other guests and cured the blasphemer for the rest of the evening.

Vulgarity

Vulgarity is obscene or lewd language that is contrary to good taste and refinement. It is always inappropriate and offensive to polite conversation. Although distasteful, vulgarity should not be confused with blasphemy. Blasphemy is abusive language directed toward God; vulgarity is abusive language that is offensive to propriety. Considering that our voice and power of communication are gifts from God, we should not abuse the gifts by using bad language, and certainly vulgarity falls into that category.

Swearing

Swearing is the taking of an oath and has nothing to do with using vulgar language. An **oath** is calling on the name of God to witness to the truth we claim to speak. This is done before a witness gives evidence in court and is referred to as "swearing in the witness." The witness is asked to raise his or her right hand and repeat the words, "I swear to tell the truth, the whole truth and nothing but the truth. . . ." Swearing is always a serious matter, but it's only sinful when we swear to a lie.

Cursing

Cursing is an invocation of evil to befall a person, place, or thing. A curse is considered an evil brought on by a higher power. But cursing is not swearing. Using the slang vernacular, "Damn you!" is cursing because we desire an to evil come to another. When used as an expletive, "Damn!" it is often an expression of frustration or anger. When one considers the consequences of being "damned," it is a good practice to eliminate this word from our language. It can be serious matter.

Perjury

Perjury, a deliberate lie said under oath, is a sin against the second commandment. This is a serious transgression against God because when the oath was taken, we called upon God to witness to what we pretended to be true. In a court of law, it is an offense against the State that can thwart justice.

Promise and Vow

A **promise** is a pledge made to do a particular act or deed. A **vow** is a solemn promise. In religious congregations, men (brothers) and women (sisters) make vows to God of poverty, chastity, and obedience. When made by monks and nuns, they are called Solemn Vows, and in non-monastic communities, they are called Simple Vows.

In the Sacrament of Matrimony, the husband and wife stand before God's minister in the presence of the church and solemnly promise God and each other to remain in an exclusive living union "until death do us part."

Promises and vows should never be made without prayerful deliberation.

The Sign of the Cross

We Catholics begin our prayers and liturgies with the Sign of the Cross. It is meant to be a sign of witness to our faith in the power of Christ's death on the cross, and at the same time, we call on the name of the Trinity as we pronounce the words, "In the *name* of the Father, and of the Son, and of the Holy Spirit. Amen." This is a holy act so don't make the Sign of the Cross in a hasty or slovenly manner. Each time we bless ourselves, we are making a call to God. We should always bless ourselves in a reverent manner.

Summary

Blasphemy is any abusive and irreverent language toward God or anything holy.

Vulgarity is obscene or lewd language that is contrary to good taste.

Swearing is taking an oath and has nothing to do with using vulgar language.

Cursing is an invocation of evil to befall a person, place, or thing.

Perjury is a deliberate lie said under oath.

A promise is a pledge made to do a particular act or deed.

A vow is a solemn promise.

The Sign of the Cross is a witness to our faith as we begin our prayers in the name of the Trinity.

3. Remember to keep holy the LORD's Day

The Jewish people observe Saturday, the seventh day of the week as the Sabbath. "The seventh day is a sabbath of complete rest, sacred to the LORD" (Ex 31:15). The Old Testament sabbath, representing the first creation, is replaced in the New Testament by Sunday, which celebrates the new creation begun in our resurrected Savior.

We Catholics keep holy the Lord's Day by participating at Holy Mass and resting from all unnecessary work. It is a violation of the third commandment for a Catholic to deliberately miss Mass on Sunday or any designated Holy Day of Obligation.

The obligation to attend Mass binds unless sickness or some serious reason prevents our attendance. Today, the vast majority of Catholics throughout the world tend to take this matter lightly since in many countries a large number do not attend Mass on a regular basis. In some European countries, attendance is astonishingly low. Has the Church changed her teaching regarding this very important obligation? No!

Some Catholics seem to think that it is not a serious matter to observe Sunday Mass, but they are wrong. The *Catechism of the Catholic Church* reminds us, "Sunday worship fulfills the moral command of the Old Covenant, taking up its rhythm and spirit in the weekly celebration of the Creator and Redeemer of his people" (2176). The same *Catechism* is even more precise a few paragraphs later, "On Sundays and other Holy Days of Obligation the faithful are bound to participate in the Mass" (2180).

Holy Mother Church has done everything possible to accommodate the faithful in observance of this commandment by allowing the obligation to be fulfilled on the vigil of Our Lord's Day, or the vigil of Holy Days of Obligation. In almost all urban parishes a Sunday-obligation Mass is offered on Saturday evening; likewise, on the evening before a Holy Day of Obligation. It's a rare set of circumstances, with the exception of illness, that the obligation cannot be met. Caring for the ill, an inaccessibility to a Catholic Church, or a legitimate dispensation from a pastor are also reasons why the faithful would be excused from Mass attendance.

Saying a Rosary, making a visit to the Blessed Sacrament, and doing acts of charity are all virtuous practices, but they do not meet the obligation to attend Mass on Sundays and Holy Days of Obligaion. This also pertains to watching a televised Mass — it's virtuous, but it does not meet the Sunday obligation. Naturally, shut-ins and patients in hospitals and nursing homes are excused from Mass attendance, but many parishes have special ministers to the sick who bring Holy Communion.

In all circumstances, we must strive to keep the Lord's Day holy and give God His day. Attending Mass translates to setting aside one hour from the 168 hours in a week to worship. That's asking very little when you think in terms of actual time. We are also obliged to set aside the Lord's Day for rest and abstain from unnecessary work.

In some instances, it may be impossible to avoid some types of work on Sundays, but it is always recommended that we keep this day special for the Lord. We have busy lives today, and because in many families both parents work, it is often difficult to avoid some chores that under different circumstances would be reserved for weekdays. Still, the faithful should sincerely attempt to reserve this day for rest and relaxation to renew them so they may better meet their obligations toward work and family.

Many Catholics reserve Sunday as "family day" and make a point to spend more time together in activities that engage every member of the family. It may be visitations to family or friends, or perhaps finding an enjoyable recreation in which all family members can participate.

Our attitude toward observing the third commandment is a good gauge for what kind of Catholics we are. The **committed Catholics** are those who have been evangelized and have a deep faith. Their attendance at Mass on Sundays as well as weekdays reflects their desire to draw closer to Our Lord. They look upon attending Mass not as an obligation, but rather as a privilege. The **habitual Catholics** do what the church commands more out of obligation than commitment. The **cultural Catholics** use the name "Catholic" mostly because they were baptized in the faith, but their observance of Mass is usually confined to special occasions and they do not practice the faith. Which type of Catholic are you?

Summary

As Catholics we observe the sabbath on Sunday, the Lord's Day.

We are bound to attend Mass on Sundays and Holy Days of Obligation.

Whenever possible we should avoid unnecessary servile work on the sabbath.

4. Honor your father and your mother

"According to the fourth commandment, God has willed that, after him, we should honor our parents and those whom he has vested with authority for our good" (2248).

The Family

The family is the nucleus of our society, and God calls us to keep that in mind in the fourth commandment. But today more than ever before, the family is under attack. Just look at the number of marriages that end in divorce and all the single parent homes that exist today. Children are even more confused if, as the victims of divorce, they witness animosity of their parents toward each other. Although we are called to "honor" our parents, it must be said that the conduct of parents should always be honorable, and that includes mutual respect for each other.

The fourth commandment focuses on respect in the family, children to respect their parents, parents to respect each other, and parents to respect their children. It is essential for parents to discipline their children, to teach them right from wrong, not only through their commands but through their example. When parents love their children discipline is present, not in terms of temporal punishment, but rather in setting down rules for the good of the whole family. That's pretty much what God had in mind when He gave us the ten commandment, and parents should teach their children from an early age that there are rules. It's good parenting and honorable to do so.

Parents are obliged to feed, clothe, and educate their children. This in not only a moral law, but it is also a law of the State. When parents fail to meet these criteria, it is harmful for the well-being of the children as well as a violation of civil law. The fourth commandment requires parents to not only provide for the temporal needs of the children, but also the spiritual. Indeed, if children are taught moral values, respect for their parents will be just one of the many benefits.

Materialism and convenience have robbed many families of a commodity that parents should be very generous with — their time. The term "quality time" has often been used when describing the relationship between parents and children, but too often "quality time" is in competition with economical or social priorities. Both the parents and the children suffer in these instances.

We have a latchkey society today, but we also have few families that are contented with a smaller home, only one automobile, only one color television, and just a few electronic items of entertainment. Computers, television, and videotape recorders have become babysitters. "Keep the kids happy, turn on a switch, and you don't have to worry about them." Not so.

Television should be viewed as a family so parents can responsibly monitor what their children are watching. If children have access to the Internet, parents have an obligation to protect them from the dangers that lurk there. And to be cautious about what movie entertainment is put before children, it's best to play it safe with "G" ratings. Even the "PG" (parental guidance) rated movies can send a lot of mixed messages to our kids. There's no electronic babysitter that can take the place of conversation and interaction between parents and children.

Because of greater longevity today, we see more and more skilled nursing facilities springing up in this country. Nursing homes serve a need, but they shouldn't be the first consideration because an aging parent has become an inconvenience. In many cases, skilled nursing is the only answer for proper care of an aged parent, but that isn't always the case. Abuse of a child is despicable, but so is abuse of a parent, and there are few scenes sadder than one finds when visiting a nursing home. Too often, aging parents are dropped off and forgotten except on birthdays and holidays. To these old folks, their families only exist in their memories, and they must turn to strangers for care and affirmation. Loneliness is probably one of the greatest sufferings shared by our aged, and how very deep must be the pain if they are parents who have children living nearby who are too absorbed in their own lives. Children of all ages are commanded to honor their father and their mother!

Authority and Obedience

Authority is most often rebelled against by people who have never learned to respect authority as children. Authority is something we live with throughout our lives, beginning with parental authority. There's also Church authority, civil authority, and authority in the workplace. God is the ultimate authority, and no authority takes priority over Him. If any authority is immoral or contrary to God's laws, we are not required to obey.

Just as we are to be respectful of authority, so too must authority be respectful of the rights of others, regardless of race, color, or creed. People in authority are obliged to base their ordinances according to God's law and moral law, or most certainly, society at large pays the consequences.

Obedience is an old fashioned word these

days. Still, there's no way we can get through this life without it. As children, we are called upon to obey our parents, teachers, elders, and anyone whom God has given the authority for our good. As adults, we must obey civil laws instituted for the welfare and protection of all citizens. As Catholics, we also have Church authority and Church teachings to obey. If we refuse to obey any of these authorities, we must suffer the consequences.

Parents have the obligation to insist upon obedience. Discipline is a loving act that produces respectful children who will learn to obey all authority providing it is not contrary to God's laws.

Whether it's civil authority or authority in the workplace that we are required to obey, we must never participate in something that may be civilly lawful but morally unlawful. A good example would be a nurse or health-care professional who must obey the medical orders of a physician, but in the case of assisting in abortion must disobey the order because it is contrary to God's commandments.

Men and women in religious orders are required to obey their superiors. Priest are bound by the rules of their bishops. Within the Church, the ultimate authority is our Holy Father.

Summary

All rightful authority comes from God.

Parents have the moral obligation to provide for the basic needs of their children as well as the spiritual needs.

Children must be taught to respect authority in the family, the Church, and society.

We are never bound by obedience to authority if it is contrary to God's laws.

5. You shall not kill

"You have heard that it was said to the men of old, 'You shall not kill: and whoever kills shall be liable to judgment.' But I say to you that every one who is angry with his brother shall be liable to judgment" (Mt 5:21-22).

Murder

Murder is the deliberate act of killing. Often when reading the Ten Commandments, many have the attitude that this commandment is one that we shouldn't have to worry about because we would never consider willfully killing anyone. But it's not that simple.

In Moral Theology the term "double effect" is used when our human act causes two simultaneous results, one good and the other evil, but only the good is desired. An example of double effect would be in the instance of a bus driver who is chauffeuring a bus load of children along a mountain pass, and as he turns the bend, a person is in his path. The only way to save the children is to proceed on his course knowing that he will hit the person with the possibility of killing him. The bus driver's intention was never to kill the innocent person in his path, but rather to save the children. Two effects resulted: the bad was the death of the pedestrian; the good was saving the children.

The act of self-defense can also have a double effect; the preservation of one's own life and the killing of the aggressor. The good effect to save one's life was desired, the bad effect of killing of the aggressor was not desired. This same rule applies to a "just war." Just as it is legitimate to defend one's own life against an unjust aggressor, so too, we may defend our nation when it is attacked in an unjust war.

Abortion

Sadly, abortion, the act of murder of an unborn child, has become lawfully acceptable here in the United States and in many other countries around the world. But God's law is very clear on this issue and is defined in the new *Catechism*: "Because it should be treated as a person from conception, the embryo must be defended in its integrity, cared for, and healed like every other human being" (2323).

In the "Didache," one of the oldest documents of the Church, the language is even more forceful: "You shall not kill the embryo by abortion and shall not cause the newborn to perish"(*Didache 2*, 2:SCh 248, 148). There's absolutely no speculation about the sin of abortion. God's laws and Church laws have remained constant, regardless of social pressures and issues disguised as "pro-choice." The teachings have not changed.

"Pro-choice" is the term used by pro-abortion people, but it is ill chosen. "Pro-murder" best describes this civilly lawful action that has become the scourge of our modern society. There are those who argue the morality of abortion, but no matter what conditions or circumstances, to take the life of an unborn child is always murder and a direct transgression against the fifth commandment, "You shall not kill," and is punishable with excommunication from the Church.

Euthanasia

Euthanasia is the act of killing with merciful intent. One might add that euthanasia is "playing God" by allowing a human being to determine when it is time to end another's life. The act of euthanasia claims to be merciful in that it eliminates suffering and pain, but just as God breathed life into us, so He should determine when our last breath is taken. The Church teaches that no matter what the motives, no matter the seriousness of the condition or handicap of the person, euthanasia is morally unacceptable.

Because euthanasia is still considered unlawful in this country, those in favor of this practice have coined a new phrase, "assisted suicide." It's meant to skirt the law and absolve the person or persons who provided the means for the victim to take his or her own life. But the act is still contrary to God's law.

Suicide

Suicide, the taking of one's own life, is forbidden by the fifth commandment. Everyone is responsible before God for the life that God has given. We are stewards, not owners, of our lives and must render an account to Him at its earthly completion. Grave psychological disturbances can diminish the responsibility of the one who takes his or her life. We should not despair of the eternal salvation of such souls since only God knows of their final destiny and we leave them to His mercy.

Health

We are responsible for the care of our physical bodies. While we should avoid the extremes of pampering or neglect, excess or deprivation, neither should we idolize physical perfection. The abuse of food, alcohol, tobacco, and drugs among others things is gravely sinful, not only to us but to those around us, especially when our excesses endanger the lives of others (for instance, drunken drivers). The fifth commandment calls us to temperance.

War

The fifth commandment also obligates all of us to work toward avoiding war. Terrorist acts against innocent civilians are always serious and sinful. There is no justification for the terrible acts of terrorism inflicted on any people throughout the world. Genocide is not only an historical event, it still happens today. In the name of "ethnic cleansing," the ugly stain of the mass murder of innocent people continues in many places throughout the world.

Summary

The fifth commandment forbids abortion and euthanasia.

We are allowed to defend ourselves and our country from attack.

We must maintain good health and not engage in any practice that is harmful to our lives or the lives of others.

6. You shall not commit adultery

The sixth commandment commands more than just fidelity between a husband and wife. It calls all of us to chastity.

Sins against chastity

Lust is a distorted desire for sexual gratification. Lustful people crave sex as an end in itself and seek it for pleasure only. Those who are lustful exercise no self-control, either of their thoughts or acts. Rather than controlling their urges, they allow their urges to control them. Lust is always seriously sinful.

Masturbation is "the deliberate stimulation of the genitals in order to derive sexual pleasure." The Church has consistently taught and "firmly maintained that masturbation is an intrinsically and gravely disordered action" (2352). This solitary act is sinful because it is selfish and not as God intended. In God's plan, the sexual act should be a triangle, male and female united in God. When one or more of these angles is missing, it is no longer the perfect act intended by our Creator. Anyone so addicted should consult a spiritual director who will give guidance according to the maturity and force of the acquired habit. Masturbation denies self-respect and abuses the gifts that God has given us to reproduce.

Fornication is sexual activities between two unmarried persons of the opposite sex. This is sinful because there is no permanent commitment and, more often than not, no real love of those involved in the intimacy. This practice is very common in the modern world, since it is claimed that two out of three high school students are no longer virgins. Even if the entire teen population were sexually active, this does not make it morally correct.

Where there is true love there will also be a desire to be joined permanently in an exclusive relationship open to life. When this total commitment is absent, it becomes a selfish act of sexual gratification where either party may leave the other at will. People who "live together" in a sexual relationship often claim that they don't need a "piece of paper" to affirm their mutual love. But Catholics, in order to enter into a sacred union, must include God in their union and profess their vows in Church to receive the grace of the sacrament.

It is most difficult for young people today when the media glorify casual sex. Catholic parents and educators have the moral responsibility to teach our youth that casual sex endangers the entire fabric of our society.

Pornography is simulated or real sex performed for the erotic excitement of a third party or parties. It is gravely sinful for the participants (actors, vendors, and public) "since each becomes an object of base pleasure and illicit profit for others" (2354). The distribution of such materials, the reading of such books, or the viewing of such imagery is gravely sinful and should be prevented by civil authority.

Prostitution is granting sex for material favors. It may be with a woman, a man, or even a child. Using children for prostitution is even more serious because it brings these children into sin and scandal. Sin is committed by the prostitute as well as the person seeking his or her services. It reduces the sexual act to nothing more than a sinful pleasure that debases God's holy gift of sexual union within the sanctity of marriage.

Rape is a most grave sin against the sixth commandment since it forces sex on unwilling parties leaving them with serious psychological wounds that can cause lifelong damage. It is graver when committed against children by relatives (incest) or by those who are responsible for the children's care. Rape is always a violent act, and violates the fifth commandment as well.

Homosexuality is a sexual desire for others of one's own sex. Being a homosexual is not sinful unless the homosexual person engages in a sex act. In other words, a homosexual person is only tempted and attracted to members of the same sex. The temptation isn't sinful, but giving in to the temptation is. Homosexuals are called to chastity just as heterosexuals are called to chastity.

The Church condemns homosexual acts as being against the natural law, and under no circumstances can they be approved. "The number of men and women who have deep-seated homosexual tendencies is not negligible. They do not choose their homosexual condition; for most it is a trial" (2358). Homosexuals must be accepted with compassion and encouraged to live chaste lives. Regardless of a person's sexual preference, we are all called to chastity.

Divorce is the legal dissolution of a marriage, but it is condemned by the Church. However, the

Church does grant annulments where there was not a validly consummated union after the marriage ceremony or between those who had an impediment at the time of the ceremony. In this case, the Church determines if either partner was psychologically, spiritually, or physically capable of entering into the sacrament. An official annulment from the Church is a decree that the union, although witnessed in the Church, was never sacramentally received.

Birth Control

"The regulation of births represent one of the aspects of responsible fatherhood and motherhood. Legitimate intentions on the part of the spouses do not justify recourse to morally unacceptable means (for example, direct sterilization or contraception)" (2399).

This teaching in the new *Catechism* is very clear and should be taken seriously. Many use the argument that the "polls" disclose that the majority of Catholics practice birth control. That doesn't make it right. The Church has always stood firm on this teaching. It has been individuals who have sought to dilute it.

Summary

Sexual union between a man and a woman is a holy gift from God reserved for the Sacrament of Marriage.

Chastity is required for all people regardless of sexual preference.

The sixth commandment calls us to respect, for ourselves and for others.

"There is no holiness without purity" (Mother Teresa).

7. You shall not steal

". . . nor thieves, nor the greedy . . . nor robbers will inherit the kingdom of God" (1Cor 6:10).

The seventh commandment doesn't just apply to the physical act of theft; it encompasses far more than that. It also urges the practice of charity and detachment from worldly possessions, and that can be quite exacting in a materialistic world. This commandment also calls us to honesty and integrity in our attitudes toward worldly possessions.

Stealing

Few of us would consider taking money from a cash register in a store, but how do we react when the clerk gives us more change back than was coming to us? Many will rationalize and say, "I spend plenty in that store; these few dollars won't make any difference to them." The point is, "it will make a difference to you." That act is stealing, taking what is not ours whether it's through the clerk's mistake or dipping our hand in the cash register and going undetected.

There's another kind of theft that most people do not look upon as stealing: Not giving an honest day's work for an honest day's pay. This is the responsibility for the employee as well as the employer. Employers have the responsibility to give a just wage, and employees have the responsibility to perform the work accordingly.

It's amusing how many people feel that cheating on income tax forms is not stealing. In the Bible we read, "Then repay to Caesar what belongs to Caesar and to God what belongs to God" (Mt 22:21). Society has a tendency to dilute this practice, claiming that, "We pay enough in taxes," or "The government has more money than I have. It won't miss it." Not good enough!

Cheating the government is cheating the common good. Tax dollars should be collected to accommodate many things; education, welfare, defense, health research, and the like, and certainly all these things effect all our citizens.

Cheating

Cheating is simply another form of theft. If a parent uses his or her wages to gamble rather than to support the family, then certainly that is stealing what should be used for the welfare of the family. With the advent of gambling boats and lotteries, many families have suffered from the indiscriminate use of money. The "get rich quick" practices have pulled apart many homes and robbed family security.

Restitution

It's not enough to be sorry that we have stolen — we must return the commodity whenever possible. When this is not possible, some other form of restitution must be made. If we have damaged another's property or possession, we must make restitution for our acts. It is our moral responsibility and is demanded by the seventh commandment.

Respect for God's Creation

God gave us dominion over all living things and the world in which we live. He has made us stewards of all creation, animate and inanimate. It is legitimate to use animals for food, and in some instance, clothing, and it is permitted to use domesticated animals for work or leisure, though we should not allow them to suffer or die needlessly.

Preservation of a healthy environment is also our responsibility. The indiscriminate destruction of forests is robbing future generations of commodities that are needed. Also, when manufacturers in the production of their products release pollutants into the air, they are robbing the community of a healthy environment.

Social Doctrine

The Church teaches that any system that reduces persons to nothing more than a means of profit is enslavement. Everyone must have the opportunity to work in order to provide for himself or herself and for the welfare of the family and community.

Any enterprise that exploits the poor by unfair wages steals the employees' right to be compensated for their work. The impact is felt not only by the individual, but by the whole community. This is most obvious in underprivileged countries where even children are used to work for pathetically low wages, thus robbing them of the advantages of higher education and better living conditions. This practice is a direct violation of the seventh commandment.

Love of the Poor

An infallible way of making restitution for our selfishness and greed is in almsgiving. This is the way to show our genuine love of the poor. The greatest example we have today of loving the poor is Mother Teresa and her sisters, who not only serve the poor, but live with them. In helping the poor, we are showing our respect for all people.

Summary

Stealing is taking something that is not rightfully ours.

Restitution must always be made when possible, or some other compensation when restitution is not possible.

We are obliged to respect all of God's creation.

We must respect the property and possessions of others.

We must strive to provide for the poor and underprivileged.

8. You shall not bear false witness against your neighbor

The eighth commandment calls us to truth. God is the source of all truth. His Word is truth. His Law is truth. We are called to be witnesses to the truth, and we have the obligation of not only speaking the truth, but searching for the truth.

Kinds of truth

Objective truth is knowing the person or fact as it really is, not as it appears. The Church has been guaranteed by Christ to speak the objective truth when teaching all that is necessary for our salvation.

Subjective truth is truth as it appears to the subject receiving it. If I believe something to be true when in fact it is not, I am not guilty of lying when I speak, even though what I believe and gave witness to is not the real truth.

Distorted truth is truth that has been slanted to fit views already held or to convince another of the distortion. For instance, suppose a reporter is covering a story and interviews a prison chaplain while at the penal institution, but when writing the story, he says, "A priest in prison, said. . . ." It gives the reader the impression that the priest is incarcerated. Obviously, a distorted truth.

The virtue of truth

We are called by the eighth commandment to be truthful in words and deeds by guarding ourselves against deceit and hypocrisy while practicing honesty and discretion. To be truthful does not mean you tell everything you know — it means expressing what ought to be expressed and keeping the rest to yourself.

Witness

Jesus witnessed to the truth before Pilate and St. Paul witnessed to the truth before his judges. As Christians, we must not be ashamed of testifying in situations that require a witness of faith. All Christians have an obligation from their baptismal promises to give witness to the faith through word and deed. That is why the Church puts so much emphasis on evangelization.

In Jesus' last recorded request in the Bible He says, "But you will receive power when the holy Spirit comes upon you, and you will be my witnesses in Jerusalem, throughout Judea and Samaria, and to the ends of the earth" (Acts 1:8). Jesus is requesting evangelization in that Scripture passage. Not all of us are free to travel to the ends of the earth, but in our own world, our neighborhood, our workplace, our socialization with others, we can evangelize our faith.

This does not mean that we should walk around with a Bible under our arm ready to quote the appropriate words and prove a point. Rather, it means through our example as loving Christians, we give witness to our faith. It also means that, whenever possible, we defend our faith to those who would speak untruths about it. This often takes courage because the fear of ridicule or unpopularity inhibits many from witnessing to the truth about matters of faith. I think it is appropriate to mention that we all have a responsibility to know our faith better so we can carry out the call to defend the faith effectively.

Martydom

Martyrdom is the supreme act of witnessing to the truth of one's faith. The martyr's death is the most powerful expression of the believer's faith. It was through the death of the early Christian martyrs that the Roman Empire was converted to Christ. The Church has always honored martyrs and recorded their heroic deeds for our inspiration and example.

Offenses against truth

False witness and perjury are publicly lying, as in a court of law or while under oath. This is not only a grave sin against the eighth commandment, it is also a criminal offense. Since one is required to ask God to witness to the truth, perjury is also a sin against the second commandment.

Rash judgment assumes as true the moral guilt of a neighbor without sufficient proof. We must never make a judgment without investigating all the facts or circumstances. For instance, if a doctor is seen leaving a brothel, to assume that he was there for sexual gratification is rash judgment. He could have been called to treat a sick person. Rash judgment is the first step to spreading scandal.

Detraction is disclosing the true faults and failings of another without an objectively good reason. To spend an hour on the phone talking about others' failures and weaknesses for the sake of gossip is sinful.

A **lie**, the most direct offense against the truth, is an untrue or inaccurate statement intended to deceive. It offends against the most fundamental right of knowing the truth. A lie can be a mortal or a venial sin depending on the gravity of the falsehood and the harm done.

Calumny causes the loss of reputation of a neighbor because the statements about them are untrue. This is the most serious form of character assassination and can cause not only the ruin of one's reputation, but also a loss of employment, alienation of others' affection, and in extreme instances may lead to suicide. The honor of our name is important, so the sins of detraction and calumny — offenses against justice and charity — are serious.

Gossip is idle conversation about another. It can also be spreading rumors without investigating truth. When one engages in gossip for the express intention of swaying someone's opinion against a third party, it is malicious and an offense against charity.

Responsibilities of the eighth commandment

Reparation must be made when one has committed an offense against justice and truth, and it should be done publicly if possible. When to speak out publicly could cause more harm, then it should be done in private.

Total reparation is difficult when a person has been the victim of malicious gossip. St. Philip Neri is reputed to have told a penitent who admitted speaking ill of another to take a bag of feathers and let them blow away in the wind. When she had completed this act she was instructed to return to him. The Saint then told her to go back and collect all the feathers that she had released. She replied, "But that is impossible, They have blown everywhere by now."

St. Philip answered, "And so have your words of gossip. All of them cannot be retrieved either."

This is a good illustration of "harmless gossip." Gossip is never harmless when the reputation of another is at stake.

Discretion must always be used in communicating information to others. Common sense and respect for the privacy, safety, and well-being of others should dictate what information we should keep to ourselves. We all have a duty to avoid scandal.

Confidentiality is important for individuals as well as professionals. It is a breach of trust to disclose information that was communicated in trust. Professionals such as clerics, political office holders, doctors, lawyers, personal secretaries, and those to whom professional secrets have been confided have a serious responsibility to keep confidences and respect the nature of the secrets entrusted to them.

The seal of confession is so sacred that it cannot be broken even under the threat of imprisonment or death. A priest can **never** refer to anything he has heard in confession, even indirectly.

Truthfulness should always be strived for when reporting a situation, whether in private or through the media. Newspapers, magazines, and television reporting have a powerful influence on society, and precaution should be taken to never distort the truth by the use of sensationalism rather than fact.

Summary

The eighth commandments calls us to always seek and convey truth.

Reparation is required when we violate truth and damage another's reputation.

Confidentiality is a breach of trust and should always be employed both privately and professionally.

9. You shall not covet your neighbor's spouse

"Everyone who looks at a woman with lust has already committed adultery with her in his heart" (Mt 5:28).

The ninth commandment calls us to purity in our thoughts as well as our actions.

78

Covetousness

To **covet** something is to excessively desire and long for something that is not ours. In the ninth commandment, it refers to **lust** and **concupiscence**, the desire for things of the flesh.

Lust and covetousness are preludes to sin and should be guarded against by being cautious about what we read and what we choose for entertainment. Anything that focuses on sexual gratification is a source of arousal and should be avoided. Each impure act begins with an impure thought.

Purity of heart

As Christians, we have the responsibility to aspire to purity of heart by wisely choosing our sources of entertainment which have broadened in the last several years. Now, along with reading material, television, and movies, we must add Internet communications. It is a well-known fact that pornographic material is readily available to the millions of people who go on-line. Parents must monitor their children's activities on their computers and alert them about the dangers of many teen chat rooms. Youthful curiosity can be a fertile field for sexual predators.

Young children are naturally pure of heart. Parents must safeguard them from being exploited as in the case of children's beauty pageants, where children are often groomed in appearance far in advance of their years. A child must not be allowed to believe that his or her self-worth is based merely on physical attributes. The innocence of a child is a precious commodity that must be protected by all parents and adults.

Modesty

Modesty should be employed in our dress as well as our actions. It is important to keep in mind that we could inadvertently be the occasion of sin for another person. We must respect our own bodies as well as the bodies of others. The forms of modesty vary with the culture of the country. In Islamic culture, it is immodest for a woman's face to go unveiled whereas in parts of Africa, it is normal for women to be publicly bare-breasted. There's a vast difference in exposing breasts where culturally acceptable and doing so solely as a matter of enticement. In the latter instance, it is always wrong.

Parents have responsibility to encourage their children to be modest in their dress, and one of the best ways is to set up guidelines regarding what is or is not acceptable. For instance, although bikinis may be popular among many teenage girls, it is up to the parents to grant permission to wear this type of attire. The argument "But everybody wears them" does not make them acceptable, especially when both boys and girls are present. Parents will be less likely to have problems dealing with this issue if they have stressed modesty in their children at an early age.

In First Corinthians chapter six, St. Paul reminds us that our bodies are temples of the Holy Spirit, and we are to glorify God with our bodies. We can never accomplish this if we attire our bodies in such a way that it could be an occasion of sin for others.

Chastity

Chastity is the virtue that tempers our sexual desires, thoughts, and actions. It demands that we not look upon others as sexual objects and promotes respect for the dignity of our own bodies as well as others' bodies.

We should strive for chastity not only as pertaining to the body, but also to the mind. Avoiding movies, TV, literature, or any media that cause sexual stimulation is a way to avoid sinful thoughts. Remember, involuntary impure thoughts are merely temptations and are not sinful, but when they are purposely pursued and entertained, then they become transgressions against the ninth commandment.

Summary

The ninth commandment forbids our entertaining any thoughts of lust.

We fortify ourselves against temptations of concupiscence through prayer and the sacraments.

We must strive for modesty and chastity in our thoughts as well as our actions.

10. You shall not covet your neighbor's goods

"For where your treasure is, there also will your heart be" (Mt 6:21).

Just as the ninth commandment forbids the inordinate desire for things of the flesh, the tenth commandment also forbids inordinate desire, but the focus is on material things. There are also other things we lust for that belong to others such as fame, power, money, and affluence. When the desire for these things results in envy, greed, or even theft, we are violating the tenth commandment as well as the seventh commandment. It is a serious sin to wish harm upon another because we are jealous and envious of their possessions or attributes.

Detachment

Detachment is the virtue of separating our-selves from worldly possessions or even relation-ships that interfere with our focus on God. It is not sinful to own things, but it is sinful to allow *things* to own us. A good way to illustrate the dif-ference is this: A conscientious Christian *loves people* and *uses things,* not *uses people* and *loves things.* We must never allow our desire to acquire worldly possessions to interfere with our spiri-tual growth.

Good will

Good will is a term that is unfortunately only heard at Christmas time, "Peace on earth, good will to men." But being of "good will" is exactly what the tenth commandment dictates because it eliminates all jealousy and envy. If we have good will, we will rejoice in our neighbor's ac-complishments, rather than resent them.

We live in a competitive society, but when the desire to win or achieve consumes us and takes our focus away from our Lord, then we are putting ourselves in the occasion of sin against the tenth commandment because we find our-selves resenting the winner or those who have excelled over us. This can happen in all areas of our lives, whether it's in academics, the workplace, sports, or any forum that creates competition.

Though we must all strive to live up to our potential and pursue our goals, we must never allow ourselves to become jealous or envious of others. This applies not only to accomplishments, but also to ownership. If we can't afford to acquire that new Cadillac or latest state-of-the-art computer, or that luxurious home we have always dreamed about, don't resent those who can.

Priorities

We must always put God first in our lives. To do otherwise is a violation of the tenth and first commandment: "Do not put strange gods before me." A strange god may be a trophy, a new car, an increase in pay, a promotion, wealth, affluence, notoriety, or praise.

Recalling one of the first catechism questions many of us learned as children will always keep our priorities straight. Why did God make us?

Answer: God made us to know Him, to love Him, and to serve Him in this world and share eternal life in the next. Anything that interferes with that purpose should never be a priority in our lives.

Summary

Wealth and fame are not in themselves sinful, but they become sinful when we regard them as a priority and more important than God in our lives.

We must strive to be detached from things of the world so we can better serve our God and attain eternal life.

Chapter Three:
The Greatest Commandment

When our dear Lord walked the earth, He was always being challenged by those who wanted to discredit Him, not unlike the way the Church is challenged today. Also, just as various movements within the Church disagree about various topics, so too did the religious factions disagree during the time of Christ. It was on one such occasion, in the twenty-second chapter of Matthew after Jesus explained the resurrection of the body after death, that the question was asked of Jesus, "Teacher, which commandment in the law is the greatest? He said to him, 'You shall love the Lord, your God, with all your heart, with all your soul, and with all your mind. This is the greatest and the first commandment. The second is like it: You shall love your neighbor as yourself. The whole law and the prophets depend on these two commandments'" (Mt 22:37).

Jesus is telling us that if we really do love God, we will automatically keep the first three, and if we really do love our neighbor, we will keep the other seven. He is telling us that love sums up the whole Bible. Love of God comes first, then love of neighbor as *yourself.*

Jesus didn't tell us we had to *like* our neighbor, He told us we had to *love* our neighbor — a big difference. Love is a decision. We may not *like* the sinner, the dictator, the murderer, the thief, the adulterer, the narcissistic person, or the person who wronged us, but we are commanded to *love* them. You might say that *liking* someone is how we feel, but *loving* someone is what we do. Jesus not only told us that we are commanded to love others; he told us *how* we should love them.

The corporal works of mercy

Our Lord wants us to respond to His love through the love we show to others. In the gospel of Matthew, Jesus says, "For I was hungry and you gave me food, I was thirsty and you gave me drink, a stranger and you welcomed me, naked and you clothed me, ill and you cared for me, in prison and you visited me" (Mt 25:35-36).

" '. . . I say to you, whatever you did for one of these least brothers of mine, you did for me' " (Mt 25:40).

The above six works of mercy are taken from the quoted Scriptural texts, but another was added, "To bury the dead," due to respect for the body as being a "temple of God, and that the Spirit of God dwells in you" (1 Cor 3:16).

All you need is love

There have been saints who were models of charity and love. St. Francis would indeed be at the top of the list. He was in tune with God's call to love and his writings reflect this, as does the "Prayer of St. Francis":

Lord, make me an instrument of your peace;
Where there is hatred, let me sow love.;
Where there is injury, let me sow pardon;
Where there is friction, let me sow union;
Where there is error, let me sow truth;
Where there is doubt, let me sow faith;
Where there is despair, let me sow hope;
Where there is darkness, let me sow light;
Where there is sadness, let me sow joy.
O Divine Master, grant that I may not so much seek to be consoled as to console,
to be understood as to understand,
to be loved as to love.
For it is in giving that we receive,
It is in pardoning that we are pardoned,
It is in dying that we are born to eternal life.

This twelfth-century friar had the formula down to the letter because he knew what it meant to really love. St. Francis was so consumed with love for our Lord that he saw the hand of God in all His creation. Even to this day, you will find statues in gardens commemorating this great saint who was a model of virtue and simplicity. To give equal time to the women who became saints, another favorite is St. Thérèse, the Little Flower. Her overwhelming love of God motivated her to write the most beautiful love letters to Jesus that still serve as devotional tools for others striving for spiritual inspiration. The Little Flower, like St. Francis, was not known for her scholarship or her oratory, but rather for her love.

Never underestimate the power of love; it's what makes heroes out of the humble, mystics out of the mundane, and saints out of the sinners. It's what keeps us going when everything else fails.

The world adapts the symbol of a heart to represent love, but the Christian uses a cross. And we Roman Catholics often use a crucifix. It's a known fact that the crucifix has been related more to Roman Catholics than any other denomination. There are those who would argue that we are a "Resurrection" people because Jesus has triumphed over the cross, and that is true. The triumph over death came from Jesus' cross, the ultimate act of love.

There are others who maintain that the image of a corpus on a cross is morbid and depressing, but what is more depressing and morbid than sin? The image of the dead Jesus represents eternal life to the Christian — that is how He earned it for us. Surely, there is nothing more uplifting than eternal life with our Father.

I remember when I was very young, one of my teachers, a nun, described Jesus' act of love on the cross, then added, "That's how much Jesus loves you, so much, that He gave His life for you. And even if you had been the only person on this earth, He would have been crowned with thorns, ridiculed, scourged, and carried His cross to the site of the place where the nails were pounded into His flesh. He would have done it all just for you." I remember being awed by that description, but like many others, the image of the cross became blurred as I grew older and the material things of this world clouded my spiritual vision. I'm certain it was through the prayers of my mother that my spiritual vision sharpened and I realized the folly in what the world had to offer. My mother spent many hours in prayer and sacrifice on my behalf because she loved me. So, don't ever quit praying for the ones you love —

it may be your prayers that save their souls.

Every few decades, God dots this earth with great lovers who remind us about His commandment to love. Today, we have a saint who personifies the corporal works of mercy — Mother Teresa. Doesn't it make you swell with pride that one of ours makes the headlines and is recognized throughout the whole world as one of the greatest lovers of our time? Her love and service to the poor, the sick, and the dying have made her a well-known figure, respected and admired by even the most hardened of hearts. This little woman, because of her response to God's love, is undoubtedly a modern-day saint. Her mission, her pledge to incorporate the corporal works of mercy wherever she goes, gives witness to her love. When she ministers to the sick and dresses their decaying flesh, or when she cradles the dying in her arms, she reminds them that they are loved. Her whole message is *God loves you.* Perhaps no other person in our times has witnessed to the power of love more dramatically and unselfishly than this little woman. Books have been written about her, documentaries have tried to characterize her mission, leaders of countries bow to her, and still she continues her work of serving the "least of my brethren," totally unaffected by the limelight. She's never distracted by the acclaim because she keeps the vision of Christ crucified before her.

Mother Teresa makes no secret of where she gets her strength, her courage, and her dedication. She says it comes from her time spent before the Blessed Sacrament in adoration. This is where she is refreshed and fortified to continue her arduous work. And here's the great news about her formula — we have the same means at our disposal too. The power of love flows from the Eucharist — it's renewed by the time we spend in His presence before the Blessed Sacrament and its rewards are peace and a knowledge that we are loved.

It's true that love is a decision, not a feeling, but it is also true that each of us needs to *feel* loved. We crave it. We need it. We flourish when we *feel* it. Perhaps, the next time when you feel lonely, isolated, or misunderstood, spend time before a crucifix and be reminded of how much you are loved. Think back about how little children sometimes illustrate how much they love by out stretching their arms. "I love you *this* much!"

Then look at the image of our dear Lord on the cross with His arms outstretched. He loves you *this* much — with nails in.

Chapter Four:

"Whose Sins You Shall Forgive"

Knowing that the devil delights in sin and despair, can you imagine how powerful the Sacrament of Penance is in spiritual warfare? Each time we receive this sacrament, we become better armed to fight the attacks of the devil, and his disguises will be ineffective as the Holy Spirit sharpens our vision through discernment and strengthens our resistance with His gifts of understanding and fortitude. You might wonder, "All this and forgiveness too?" But friends, that's how it works.

When we confess our sins to a priest, we not only receive absolution — forgiveness — we also receive the grace of the sacrament. In simple terms, grace is divine assistance in helping us to grow closer to God. We are always urged to take advantage of this powerful sacrament, and although it is an absolute necessity if we have committed a mortal sin, it is also a great tool to overcome our weaknesses that lead to venial sin.

The Church now refers to confession as the Sacrament of Reconciliation because through sin we separate ourselves from God, and in receiving forgiveness and having contrition, we are reconciled with Him and the Church once again. The practice of going to confession has been a stumbling block for many non-Catholics who claim to admire our Church and at times even aspire to becoming a Catholic, but they can't accept the practice of confessing their sins to another human being. That's a modern-day problem, but it also existed during the time of Christ.

The second chapter of Mark illustrates the controversy about the power to forgive sins even back then. If you recall, we read in that chapter that Jesus returned to Capernaum and the news of His preaching and healing preceded Him, so crowds gathered to hear Him. Four men carrying a paralytic couldn't enter through the crowded doorway, so they lowered the man on a mat through the roof. Jesus recognized their faith and told the paralytic that his sins were forgiven.

The scribes immediately began to deliberate among themselves and questioned Jesus' power to forgive sins. They believed that Jesus was blaspheming because they maintained that only God could forgive sins. but Jesus read their minds so He asked them which was easier to believe, that He could tell the paralytic that his sins were forgiven, or if He told him to pick up his mat and walk. To prove to the onlookers, especially those questioning the power to forgive sins, Jesus told the man to rise, pick up his mat, and go home. Immediately, the paralyzed man followed Jesus' instructions and walked away as all who were gathered watched. Jesus displayed the power to forgive sins in a very dramatic way by healing the paralyzed man. No one questioned that power when they saw a physical healing because they witnessed a miracle with their own eyes. Times haven't changed. People who question a priest healing souls have no qualms about going to a faith healer for their sick bodies.

To those who still protest against the practice of confessing our sins to a priest, it is important to refer to another place in Scripture in the twentieth chapter of John, and note that within the very first few minutes that Jesus revealed Himself in His resurrected state, He passed this power to forgive sins to His followers. The frightened apostles were gathered together behind locked doors when Jesus appeared to them and greeted them with "Peace be with you." Then He showed them His hands and side. We are told that the apostles rejoiced at the sight of their Master. But our dear Lord then bestowed on them a special power after He once again said, "Peace be with you." It was at that moment He breathed on them and said, "Receive the Holy Spirit. If you forgive men's sins, they are forgiven; if you hold them bound, they are held bound." It's more than symbolic that His greeting of peace and the gift to forgive sins are in the same text, because only through forgiveness will we have peace.

Thomas wasn't present when this occurred, and when the other apostles tried to convince him that it really happened, Thomas announced that he would never believe without probing the nail prints in Jesus' hands and putting his hand into Jesus' side. I have always thought it was interesting that Thomas was so graphic about his disbelief when choosing the wounds that Christ endured for our sins to be shown as proof that Jesus appeared to the other followers. But Jesus held Thomas at his word when he later appeared to him and told Thomas to take his finger and examine His hands then to put his finger into His side.

When Thomas saw Jesus with his own eyes, he responded with the same words that many of us use after the words of consecration in the Mass, "My Lord and my God!" That's very significant, since many a doubting Thomas also questions the real presence of Jesus in the Eucharist.

Of all the sacraments, Penance and the Eucharist are the two sacraments that we may receive as often as we need or desire. Baptism, Confirmation, Holy Orders, and Matrimony are received only one time in our lives with the exception of a widower who later becomes a priest; then he would have received both Matrimony and Holy Orders. The Sacrament of the Sick may be received more often, but it is really not as readily available to us as Penance and the Eucharist. With the life-giving grace of these two sacraments being at our advantage whenever we choose, it's no wonder that these two sacraments are challenged the most by non-believers. These two sacraments are strong armament against the attacks of the devil.These are the two sacraments for which we need a priest exclusively (Read 2 Cor 5:11-21 on the ministry of reconciliation).

If anyone has any doubts about the spiritual warfare going on in our contemporary world, there is evidence in the fact that attitudes and practices have changed so dramatically in the past three decades. If you're over forty, you can probably remember when there was a line outside the confessional on Saturday evenings. The lines became shorter and shorter and unfortunately in some parishes now, confession is only available by appointment. *Where have all the sinners gone?*

They're still out there, but the fact that there are fewer confessions today is visible in two reasons often used by Catholics. The first questions the power of the priest to forgive sin: "Ater all, he is a sinner too." And the second reason for not going to confession is the belief that they have no sins to confess. "Nobody calls it *sin* anymore."

We have addressed the power to forgive sins through the Scriptures, but convincing the second group of people who believe they have no sin is a bit more complicated. Somewhere in the people's spiritual formation, they absolved themselves of their transgressions and forgot about the power they can receive through frequent reception of the Sacrament of Penance.

I once had a discussion with a very liberal religious education teacher who told me that too much emphasis on the practice of going to confession results in scrupulosity. But the people who suffer from this malady usually have the misbelief that God is sitting in heaven with a big score sheet eager to give us a bad mark. I have also found that many are motivated by reward and punishment rather than accepting the loving mercy of God. There has to be balance for a healthy soul.

We all want peace in our lives, and the first place to look is inside ourselves. We Catholics have a distinct advantage because the forgivenss and grace of the Sacrament of Reconciliation is there for us. Take advantage of it. *Peace be with you!*

Examination of Conscience

If we have strived to form a good conscience, we already recognize our sins and weaknesses, but in the formation of our spiritual lives, it is good to frequently examine our conscience by reviewing the Ten Commandments. Although we have studied the Ten Commandments more thoroughly in the preceding pages, we now apply them more personally to our own lives.

1. I am the LORD, your God, you shall not have strange gods before me.

Is God first in my life? What do I spend most of my waking moments thinking about? What is the most important thing in my life? Pleasure? Food? Money? Sports? Do I spend as much time thinking about God as I do of these other things? What about my prayer life? If I only ate food as often as I pray, how hungry would I be? Is the practice of my Faith important to me? Have I taken part in witchcraft or superstitious practices?

2. You shall not take the name of the LORD, your God in vain.

Do I respect the Holy name of God? Do I profane anything sacred? Have I become careless regarding the use of God's name in conversation?

3. Remember to keep holy the LORD's Sabbath.

Have I missed Mass on Sunday through my own fault? Have I deliberately missed Mass on any Holy Day of Obligation? Have I really tried to make the Lord's Day special?

4. Honor your father and your mother.

Have I shown the proper respect for my parents? Have I shown the proper respect for my children? Have I been respectful of people who have authority over me?

5. You shall not kill.

Have I supported abortion? Do I regard violence as an acceptable form of media entertainment? Have I knowingly inflicted pain — physical or emotional — on someone else? Do I respect the right to life for the unborn?

6. You shall not commit adultery.

Have I engaged in sexual activity alone or with anyone outside of marriage? Have I watched and enjoyed pornography? Have I deliberately dressed to entice someone else? Do I really consider my body and the bodies of others as "temples of the Holy Spirit"?

7. You shall not steal.

Have I deliberately taken something that is not mine? Have I cheated an employer? Have I given an honest day's work for an honest day's pay? Have I paid people justly and according to their labor? Have I respected others' property and possessions? Have I cheated?

8. You shall not bear false witness against your neighbor.

Have I engaged in idle gossip? Have I deliberately lied? Have I knowingly sought to destroy someone's reputation?

9. You shall not covet your neighbor's spouse.

Have I lusted for another's spouse? Have I entertained impure thoughts and desires by allowing them to entertain me? Have I avoided sensuous literature, movies, or conversations that I know will result in sexual arousal?

10. You shall not covet your neighbor's goods.

Do I envy others' good fortune? Am I jealous of others' position or fame? Am I jealous and envious that I don't possess the same possessions or traits that others have?

Making a good confession

We now have the option of receiving the Sacrament of Penance either through the screened confessional or face to face. The choice is yours according to which you prefer. To make a good confession, we must first have sincere contrition, genuine sorrow for our sin, contempt for the sin we have committed, and a firm resolve to avoid the sin in the future.

The new *Catechism* as well as the old *Baltimore Catechism* teach that there are two kinds of contrition, perfect and imperfect. Perfect contrition is sincere sorrow for offending God whom we love with our whole heart and soul. Imperfect contrition is sorrow for our sins because we fear God's punishment or the consequences of our sin. Though either contrition qualifies as a good confession, it is easy to discern that perfect contrition is held by those who have a more intimate relationship with our Lord. It is motivated by love more than fear.

When we enter the screened confessional or sit before the priest face to face, we should first acknowledge our sin. "Bless me, Father, for I have sinned. It is _____ since my last confession." To give the priest insight and to allow the penitent to make a quick spiritual inventory, it is recommended that the penitent state when he or she last received the sacrament. Then it is time to confess our sins, and if you need help or have any questions at all, discuss them with the priest.

Remember the priest is there for you, to extend to you the forgiveness of your sins as God's official minister of the sacrament. He is not there to judge you — that is reserved for God alone. And never worry about the priest keeping your confidence. He is bound by serious sin to keep the confidentiality of the penitent. If you're afraid of being embarrassed, I hasten to remind you that it is doubtful that you have anything to confess that the priest hasn't heard before.

When you have finished confessing your sins, the priest directs you to make a sincere act of contrition, gives you "a penance," then administers absolution.

Why the penance? "The confessor proposes the performance of certain acts of 'satisfaction' or 'penance' to be performed by the penitent in order to repair the harm caused by sin and to reestablish habits befitting a disciple of Christ" (1494).

There are a number of "acts of contrition" prayers that express sorrow for our sins and resolve not to commit them again available, but not one of them is officially prescribed. You can choose your own words that express sorrow, the desire to be reconciled with God, and your resolve to avoid sin in the future.

Born Again

In the Sacrament of Penance, your sins are not only forgiven, they are taken away. You are born again, free to start all over in your desire to grow closer to God. Sin no longer separates you from God, and if you have made a sincere confession, you will have peace (read 2 Cor 5:16-21).

I strongly recommend that, after making a good confession, the penitent takes time to spend alone with our Lord. Feel His Divine Presence. Rejoice in His love. Respond to His call.

"As the Father loves me, so I also love you. Remain in my love" (Jn 15:9).

Chapter Five:
"My Peace I Leave You"

As their priest and counselor, people have shared with me the sorrows and concerns that complicate their lives, and invariably they will state, "All I want is peace, Father." Peace is that elusive commodity that everybody is seeking in this world but seldom finds. Too often they are confusing peace with comfort or freedom from problems. If peace is really what we seek, we need only to claim the legacy that Jesus gave us. "Peace I leave with you; my peace I give to you. Not as the world gives it to you" (Jn 14:27).

This world can never satisfy our need for peace because we judge peace by human standards. Life brings pain, sorrow, misunderstanding, disappointments, hurt, betrayal, and confusion, but if we accept Jesus' legacy to us, we will still know peace. I've seen it over and over again in a mother who has lost a child, in a wife or husband who has lost a spouse, in the terminally ill, and even in the sick person who is anguished in pain. Despite all the hurtfulness, there is a quiet peace because they look beyond what this world has to offer. "As we look not to what is seen but to what is unseen; for what is seen is transitory, but what is unseen is eternal" (2 Cor 4:18).

Following Jesus and keeping God's commandments will not protect us from the pain and troubles of this world, but it will allow us to keep our priorities straight. We will be better equipped to recognize those things that can lead us to sin and the separation from God. In today's world, that is not such a simple task since sin has been camouflaged by the pursuit of pleasure, not happiness; by comfort, not peace; by fame, not humility; by fortune, not charity; by ambition, not love; and by confusion, not faith.

Though this book has tried to expose sin and the devastation it brings, its purpose is not merely to define sin. I would like to think it's a book about love, peace, and mercy. "For God so loved the world that he gave his only Son, so that everyone who believes in him might not perish but might have eternal life" (Jn 3:16).

Back in the seventies, there was a popular bumper sticker that read, "Smile, God loves You!" It was downright profound, but not many took it seriously. Still there are volumes written about that message. Indeed, that is the Good News, *God loves you!* Perhaps many of us never take enough time out to really meditate and grasp these words, but if you ask God's help in realizing His love,

He'll help you. Then gaze upon a crucifix to fathom that Love even more. Know that you are loved so that you can better understand God's first commandment, ". . . 'You shall love the Lord, your God, with all your heart, with all your soul, and with all your mind' " (Mt 22:37).

St. Catherine of Siena, who was declared a Doctor of the Church by Pope Paul VI in 1970, was also considered one of the finest theological minds in the Church. Among her writings and in just a few lines, she captured what this whole book has been about.

"He who knows himself to be loved cannot do otherwise than love. In loving he will put on the spirit of Christ crucified, and in the tempestuous sea of many troubles, he will find himself at peace."

Epilogue

During the writing of this book, I was asked by a few people what my new book was about. Whenever I told them the title, *Nobody Calls It Sin Anymore*, invariably they would comment, "That's good, Father; it's about time," or "Great; I don't think our young people even know what sin is." Naturally, I was encouraged by the enthusiasm for a book such as this, a book that reminds people that sin does exist. But this is also a book about healing.

No one will question that we are healed when we are forgiven for our sins, but we must remember that we can't be completely healed unless we are also ready to forgive. When praying the Our Father, we ask God to "forgive us our trespasses, as we forgive those who trespass against us," but do we really mean it? Do we want God to extend His forgiveness to us in the same quantity that we extend forgiveness to others? I doubt it.

One of the reasons that many do not take advantage of the Sacrament of Reconciliation is that they can't imagine being forgiven since they have been unable to forgive. But if we obey the greatest commandment, to love God with our whole heart, our whole mind, and our whole soul, and to love our neighbors as ourselves, we must be ready to forgive. And we must not only pray to receive mercy, we must pray for the grace to extend mercy. It's not easy.

Left to ourselves and our own power, we will surely fail. But through meditating on Christ's ultimate act of love, His crucifixion, we find that transgressions against us pale in comparison. Who among us has been scourged, crowned with thorns, made to carry a heavy cross, only to be nailed to it and left to die? After suffering all that, Jesus prayed to His Father and begged forgiveness on our behalf. ". . . 'Father, forgive them, they know not what they do' " (Luke 23:34).

Our Lord was not only begging forgiveness for His persecutors; He was asking His Father's mercy for each one of us. God answered His Son's prayer for us. His forgiveness and mercy is ours when we claim it through the Sacrament of Reconciliation, and nourish it through the Eucharist.

This is not so much a book about sin, but a book about God's love and mercy. God has given us all we need to have eternal life. That's the good news. So smile. *God loves you!*

Our Sunday Visitor...
Your Source for Discovering the Riches of the Catholic Faith

Our Sunday Visitor has an extensive line of materials for young children, teens, and adults. Our books, Bibles, booklets, CD-ROMs, audios, and videos are available in bookstores worldwide.

To receive a FREE full-line catalog or for more information, call **Our Sunday Visitor** at **1-800-348-2440**. Or write, **Our Sunday Visitor** / 200 Noll Plaza / Huntington, IN 46750.
